SCIENCE GOES TO THE DOGS

SCIENCE GOES TO THE DOGS

CARTOONS BY S. Harris
FOREWORD BY Isaac Asimov

Philadelphia

Published by

iSi PRESS® A Subsidiary of the
Institute for Scientific Information®
3501 Market St., University City Science Center, Philadelphia, PA 19104 U.S.A.

ISBN 0-89495-043-6

Printed in the United States of America
90 89 88 87 86 85   8 7 6 5 4 3 2 1

Table of Contents

For Jennifer and Jonathan,
who can take dogs or leave them

FOREWORD

What is humor? I'm in no mood to be learned about it. I don't wish to become very abstract, and to generalize. I don't want to seek for the fundamental basis of the ludicrous, the comic, the funny.

I am, instead, going to be very scientific and give "humor" an operational definition. I won't tell you what it *is*; I will tell you how it can be *identified*.

Here it is! . . . Humor is what makes me laugh. If I laugh in any way; if I snicker, chuckle, guffaw, or go into hysterics, that which has induced it is funny.

Of course you may say, "But it doesn't make *me* laugh."

Well, don't boast about it. I have long ago come to the conclusion that people who don't laugh at what makes me laugh have no sense of humor and should be ashamed of themselves. On the other hand, if they laugh at what doesn't make me laugh, they are peculiar, and ought not foist themselves on normal people.

There! I think the matter is settled to everyone's (i.e. *my*) satisfaction, and we can get on to the nub of the matter.

Sidney Harris is funny.

What's more, his humor is particularly delightful because it is unique. No one else mines quite the vein of fun that he does. If he didn't draw his cartoons, no one in the world would produce anything even faintly like them.

For instance, he has virtually patented the funny-science cartoon. If you ever see a cartoon of Albert Einstein staring at the equation $e = mb^2$ on the blackboard and shaking his head in bewilderment, you'll know that Harris drew it. If you look a little to one side, you will see me in hysterics, because I know what the equation should *really* be.

Now Harris has found himself another way of being successfully ludicrous. We all know (i.e. *I* know) that one way of seeing something with sudden luminous clarity is to look at it from another vantage point.

For instance, have you ever thought of looking at the world—at society—at psychiatry—at common assumptions—from a dog's point of view? Better yet, looking at it all from Sidney Harris's *notion* of a dog's point of view?

Find his cartoon showing the difference between left-brain dominance and right-brain dominance, and you will laugh at once if you are as decent a human being as I am. You may even decide that you now have a new insight into the problem and that you may never be able to take it with quite the frowning seriousness that psychologists want you to. Ditto, ditto, the doggish difference between extraversion and introversion, the blind dog's version of a seeing-eye *what*; and so on.

Leaf through this book and be prepared to laugh joyously at Sidney Harris's peculiar and special sense of fun, and (just possibly) see the world as you've never seen it before.

ISAAC ASIMOV

Science Goes to the Dogs

ISAAC NEWTON DISCOVERS THE LAW OF GRAVITY

ONE-CELLED DOG

SPECIES: A SINGLE, DISTINCT KIND OF PLANT OR ANIMAL HAVING CERTAIN DISTINGUISHING CHARACTERISTICS.

BIG BARK THEORY
(CANINE VERSION OF THE ORIGIN OF THE UNIVERSE)

EVOLUTION

LOUIS PASTEUR
AND HIS
RABID DOG

BRAIN TRANSPLANT

AIR BAG

PARTICLE ACCELERATOR   DOG ACCELERATOR

FOOD CHAIN

IDENTICAL TWINS   FRATERNAL TWINS

PROTOPLASM

PHOSPHORUS + SULPHUR + CARBON +
OXYGEN + HYDROGEN + CALCIUM +
NITROGEN + IRON =

CANINE TECHNOLOGY

BRAIN

MOON DOG HOWLING AT EARTH

STATE-OF-THE-ART DOG

PET SHOP

14024 14282

THE FOUR BASIC FOOD GROUPS

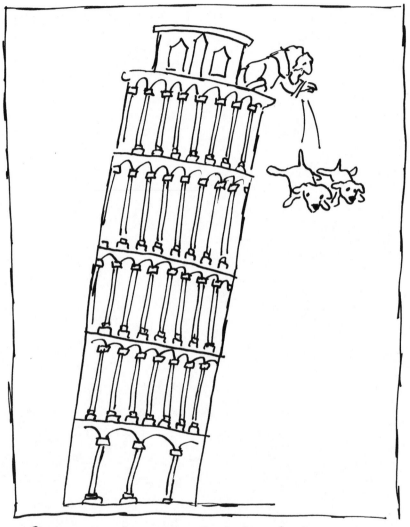

GALILEO'S ATTEMPT TO DISCOVER IF
HEAVIER DOG FALLS FASTER THAN
LIGHTER DOG.

PERPETUAL MOTION

The Social Sciences

28

RANDOM SAMPLE

GRAFFITI

EXTROVERT   INTROVERT

CLAUSTROPHOBIA

BEHAVIOR MODIFICATION

MULTIPLE PERSONALITIES

PECKING ORDER   PECKING OUT-OF-ORDER

Dyslexia

IDENTITY CRISIS

PERTINENT DOG

GERMANE SHEPHERD

LEFT BRAIN DOMINANCE

RIGHT BRAIN DOMINANCE

SELF-ACTUALIZATION

FREE-ASSOCIATING

BALANCED TICKET

FACTS OF LIFE

TAX LOOPHOLE:
PUTTING EVERYTHING IN THE DOG'S NAME

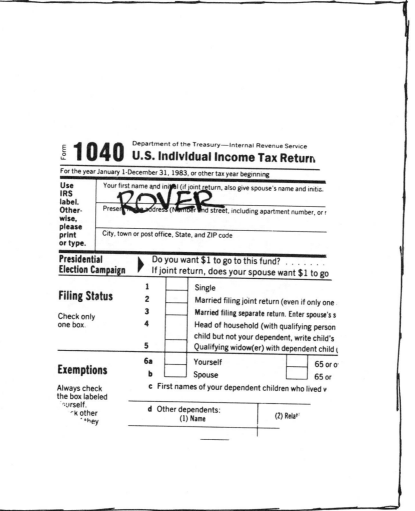

THE MONGREL MAJORITY

Math and Logic

SOLID GEOMETRY DOG

PLANE GEOMETRY DOG

$DOG^2 =$

PROBABILITY

IF YOU HAVE 5 DOGS, 3 WILL
BE ASLEEP

A-A-B-A

Literature and the Arts

WOOFGANG AMADEUS MOZART

HEMINGWAY'S DOG MEETS FAULKNER'S DOG

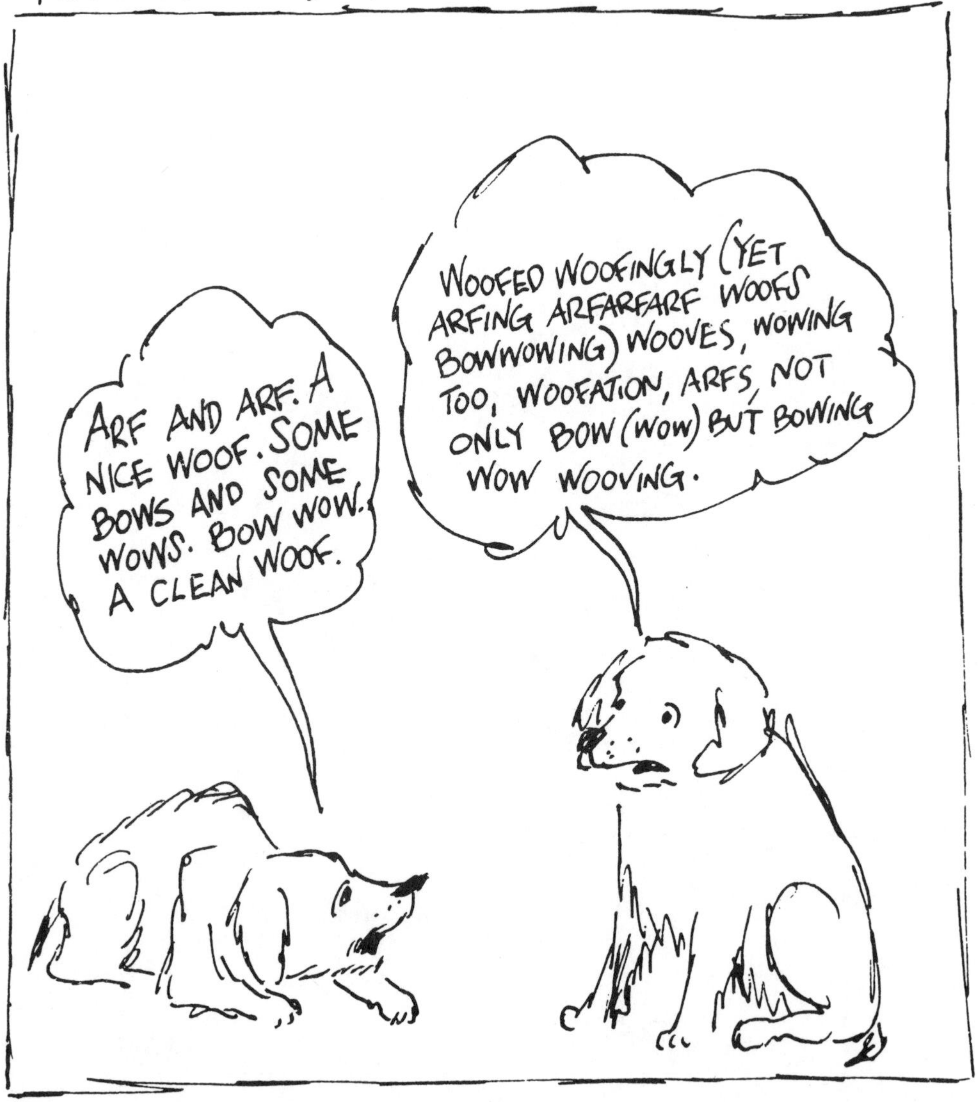

LEONARDO DA VINCI'S DOG

MARIE ANTOINETTE UPDATE

SHAKESPEARE'S LOST PLAY:
THE TAMING OF THE POOCH

As the night followest the day,
You shall follow my heel...

GRAMMARIAN

PALINDROME DOG

"DALMATIAN? NA! IT AM LAD."

DOG DICTIONARY

ARF
BOW-WOW
WOOF

DOG ALPHABET

A
B
F
O
R
W

SCAT SINGING   SDOG SINGING

72

UPON DISCOVERING THAT 'DOG' CAN
BE USED AS A DEROGATORY TERM.

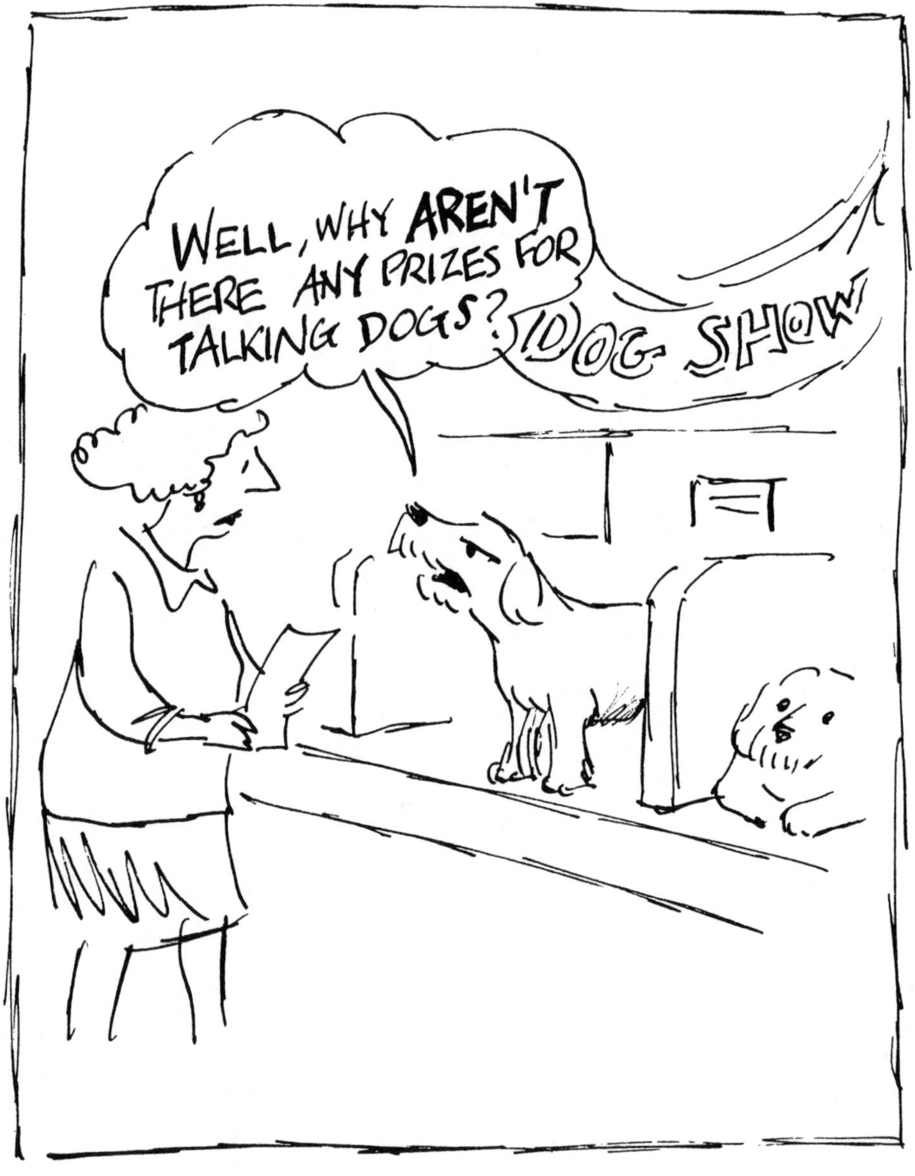
WELL, WHY AREN'T THERE ANY PRIZES FOR TALKING DOGS?
DOG SHOW

LONG-RANGE PLANNING

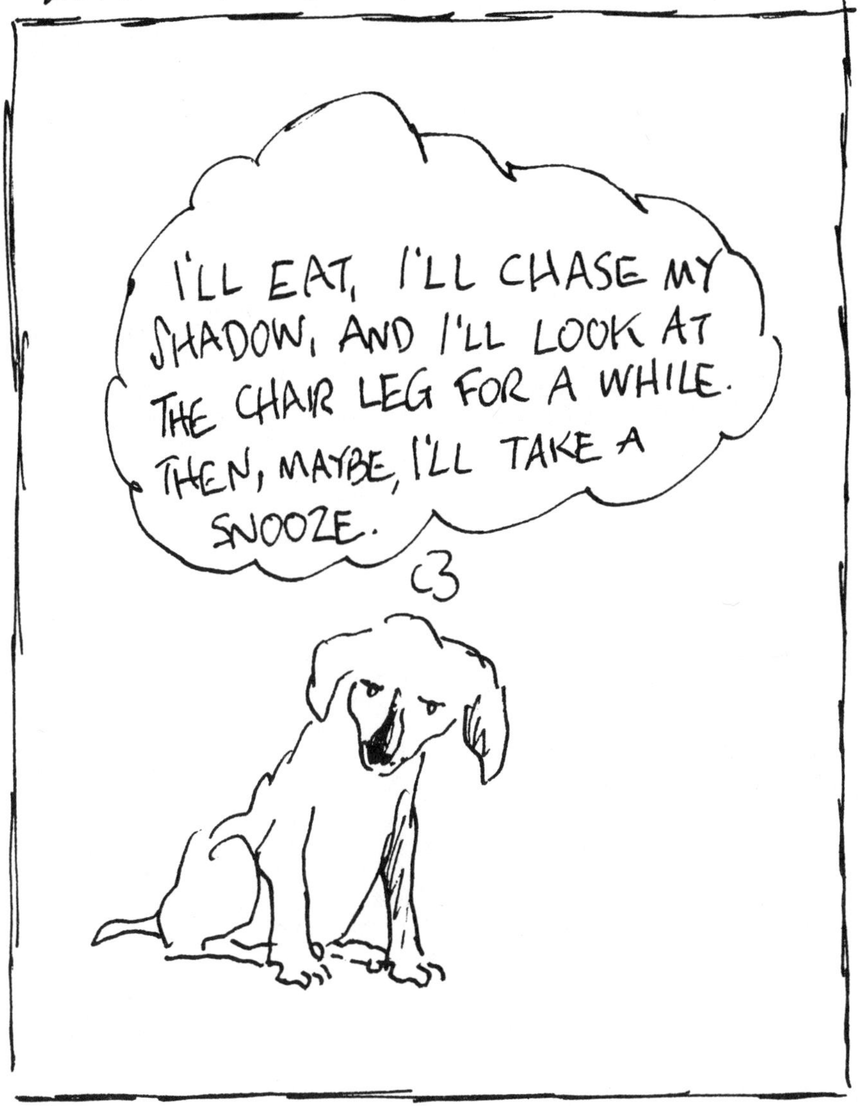

MEASURE OF DEVOTION!
$5 REWARD FOR LOST DOG

PEDIGREED DOG   GENERIC DOG

Collie, F, 4 yrs. old, well-trained, Knows many tricks, wants to meet M, collie, afghan, or greyhound. No mutts, please.

DOG WITH ALL THE HAIR HE HAS EVER SHED

BARKS IN CODE

It's a Dog's Life

SIGHT-IMPAIRED DOG

FLOWCHART

ABOMINABLE SNOW DOG

SPOT · SPOTLESS

The Four Freedoms

Freedom to Bark
Freedom from Fetching
Freedom to Sleep on Any Piece of Furniture
Freedom from Leashes

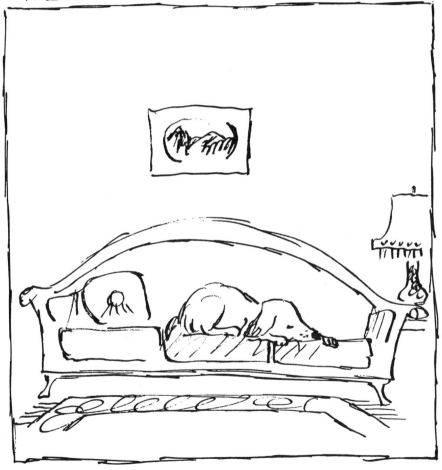

DOG DAY AFTERNOON

WINNERS: 100 YARD AUTOMOBILE CHASE

JUNK FOOD FOR DOGS

FAST FOOD FOR HUMAN AND PET

Conclusions

DESCARTES' DOG

ZEN

DOGENES

LOOKING FOR AN HONEST CANINE

IF A DOG BARKS IN THE FOREST, AND
NO ONE HEARS HIM, DOES HE MAKE A SOUND?

COLLECTIVE UNCONSCIOUS

MAN'S BEST
FRIEND

MAN'S WORST
FRIEND

MAN'S ONLY
FRIEND

INTROSPECTION

THE MEANING OF LIFE